Contents

Introduction

The continent of Antarctica includes areas of rocky hills and mountains.

Mapping the world

Exploration takes many forms: the search for trade, the urge to find new lands to conquer, the pursuit of science, the quest for other knowledge. By the late 19th century, most of the world had been discovered and claimed, and there were few areas left on the map that had not yet been visited by human beings.

There were two exceptions: the extreme north and the extreme south of the earth. Over several hundred years, navigators and explorers had started to develop a picture of these places as they searched for sea routes. They brought back tales of the extreme cold, and of landscapes covered in thick layers of ice. Many people lost their lives in these hostile places, and there seemed to be little of value there besides whales and seals — little worth the risks involved.

For glory

In 1876, this expedition came to within 600 kilometres of the North Pole.

By the final years of the 19th century the challenge of these last great blank spaces on the map was too great to resist. Scientists and mapmakers wanted to know what was at the very top and bottom of the earth, and there were people who were prepared to risk the extreme dangers to find out. They had to be exceptionally tough, very well organised, and determined almost to the point of obsession. At the end of gruelling months of battling against terrible cold, exhaustion, disease, isolation and the constant threat of starvation lay the great prize: the satisfaction of being the first person to stand at the North or the South Pole.

PEARY AND AMUNDSEN
Race to the Poles

Antony Mason

Evans Brothers Limited

Evans Brothers Limited
2A Portman Mansions
Chiltern Street
London
W1M 1LE

Printed in Hong Kong

ISBN 0 237 51451 6

Series editor: Su Swallow
Editor: Nicola Barber
Consultant: Robert Headland,
   Scott Polar Research Institute, Cambridge
Designer: Ken Brooks
Production: Jenny Mulvanny

Illustrations: Brian Watson, Linden Artists

Acknowledgements

For permission to reproduce the following material the author and publishers gratefully acknowledge the following:

Front cover (top left) Eskimo life – Peter Newark's Historical Pictures, (top right) musk ox – Johnny Johnson, Bruce Coleman Limited, (middle) Eskimo mask – Walter Rawlings, Robert Harding Associates, (bottom left) Eskimo artefacts – Bruce Coleman, (bottom right) emperor penguins – Hans Reinhard, Bruce Coleman Limited.
Title page Roger Mear, Royal Geographical Society
Page 4 (top) Francisco J. Erize, Bruce Coleman Limited, (bottom) Royal Geographical Society **page 5** Royal Geographical Society **page 7** (left) Erwin & Peggy Bauer, Bruce Coleman Limited, (right) Francisco J. Erize, Bruce Coleman Limited **page 9** e.t. archive **page 11** Peter Newark's Historical Pictures **page 12** (top) Royal Geographical Society, (bottom) Mary Evans Picture Library **page 13** Roger A. Coggan, Bruce Coleman Limited **page 14** (top) Royal Geographical Society, (bottom left) Norman D. Price, (bottom right) Leonard Lee Rue III, Bruce Coleman Limited **page 15** Royal Geographical Society **page 16** (left) E. & D. Hosking, Frank Lane Picture Agency, (right) Popperfoto **page 18** Royal Geographical Society **page 19** (top) Hulton Deutsch Collection Limited, (bottom) Popperfoto **page 20** Royal Geographical Society **page 22** Royal Geographical Society **page 23** (left) Range, Bettmann, (right) Radio Times Hulton Picture Library **page 24** Scott Polar Research Institute, Robert Harding Associates **page 25** Roger Mear, Royal Geographical Society **page 26** Hulton Deutsch Collection Limited **page 27** (top) Paul Popper, Robert Harding Picture Library, (bottom) Popperfoto **page 28** (top) Royal Geographical Society, (bottom) Roald Amundsen Museum, Robert Harding Picture Library **page 29** Geoff Renner, Robert Harding Picture Library **page 31** (left) Royal Geographical Society, (right) M. Reitz, The Image Bank **page 32** (top) Roger Mear, Royal Geographical Society, (bottom) Paul Popper, Robert Harding Picture Library **page 33** Popperfoto **page 34** (top) Roger Mear, Royal Geographical Society, (bottom) Popperfoto **page 35** Hulton Deutsch Collection Limited **page 36** Fred Bruemmer, Bruce Coleman Limited **page 37** (top) Walter Rawlings, Robert Harding Associates, (bottom) Erwin & Peggy Bauer, Bruce Coleman Limited **page 38** (top) Wally Herbert Collection, Robert Harding Associates, (middle) Walter Rawlings, Robert Harding Associates, (bottom) Norman D. Price **page 39** Leonard Lee Rue III, Bruce Coleman Limited **page 40** (top) Royal Geographical Society, (bottom) Dr Sabine M. Schmidt **page 41** Royal Geographical Society **page 42** Stephen J. Krasemann, Bruce Coleman Limited **page 43** Dr David Millar, Science Photo Library.

Robert Peary (right) was 53 years old when he made his final attempt to reach the North Pole in 1909.

Roald Amundsen (far right) was one of the most experienced polar explorers when he set out on his expedition to the South Pole in 1910.

Horizons

After reading this book, you may want to find out more about the many polar explorers whose expeditions helped to make the achievements of Peary and Amundsen possible, and whose work has contributed to our knowledge of the Arctic and Antarctic today. At the end of some of the chapters in this book you will find **Horizons** boxes. These boxes contain the names of people who made major contributions to polar exploration. By looking up these names in the indexes of other reference books, you will discover a great deal more fascinating information.

The general public followed these expeditions with increasing interest, and they were reported widely in the newspapers. The first explorers to reach each Pole could expect to be rewarded for all their hardships with fame and glory. Above all else, it was this quest for fame — to be the first to the Poles — that drove the American, Robert Peary, and the Norwegian, Roald Amundsen. 'I *must* have fame', wrote Peary, early in his long career of Arctic exploration. But the path to fame was as hazardous and treacherous as the path across the frozen wastes to the Poles. Both Peary and Amundsen were meticulous planners, and their success depended upon it. However, what neither explorer had planned was the lukewarm reception he received when each claimed his hard-earned victory. In both cases, events were to cheat the explorers of the full glory to which they believed themselves entitled.

For science and knowledge

It would be wrong, however, to think that all polar explorers were driven by glory. Some needed the prospect of glory to give them the determination to push themselves to the limits of endurance. Others travelled in search of knowledge: they wanted to find out more about these mysterious wildernesses, how they were formed, how their weather affects the weather patterns of the world, how their wildlife survives, how the human body copes in such conditions. Peary and Amundsen were both part of a great tradition of polar exploration which set out to answer these and other questions, a tradition that has survived until this day, and that still calls upon men and women to face the hardships and the life-threatening cold to study the unique lessons of the far ends of the earth.

The historical background

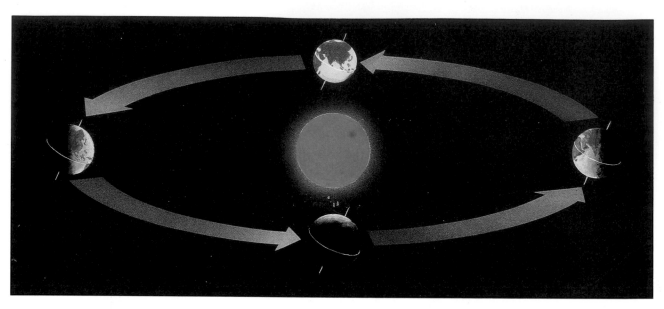

The Earth's orbit around the Sun. When it is winter in the southern hemisphere (left) it is summer in the northern hemisphere. When it is summer in the southern hemisphere (right) it is winter in the north.

Polar nights and midnight sun

The regions at the far north and far south of the earth are extremely cold because they are never sufficiently warmed by the sun. Because of the round shape of the earth, the sun's rays have further to travel to reach the polar regions than the Equator. What is more, the rays hit the polar regions at an angle, and they are reflected away by the white snow and ice. As a result, the Poles are the coldest places on earth. Temperatures are rarely above freezing point (0°C), and often reach -40°C. A record low temperature of -89°C has been recorded in Antarctica.

As it orbits around the sun, the earth is also revolving. The line around which the earth revolves is called its axis. The earth's axis tilts over at an angle from the upright of about 23°. This small tilt is what causes the seasons on earth, and it means that winter days become shorter the further north or south you go from the Equator. In the polar regions, the sun is not seen at all for about ten weeks during the winter. During this 'polar night', temperatures are at their lowest. By contrast, in midsummer the sun never sets in polar regions; it makes a complete turn around the horizon giving 24 hours of sunlight — the 'midnight sun'.

The Poles are at the opposite ends of the world's two hemispheres, so when it is summer in the Arctic, it is winter in the Antarctic.

Both the Arctic and Antarctica are covered by ice. But in geological terms the two extremes of the earth could not be more different. The Arctic is a frozen ocean, and the North Pole sits on a layer of ice over seawater. Antarctica is a continent, a huge piece of land bigger than Australia. Not much is known about this land because it is covered with a coating of ice, on average two kilometres thick. Antarctica has mountains rising to almost 5000 metres, and the South Pole itself is on a plateau almost 3000 metres high.

At a temperature of -1.8°C sea water freezes, so as winter advances the area of ice around the polar regions expands. In the Arctic, the icecap advances across the sea to join up with the surrounding landmasses of northernmost Canada, Alaska, Russia, Norway and Greenland. In Antarctica a huge area of sea freezes in the winter, covering an area almost as large as the continent itself. Water expands as it freezes, so the advancing icecaps are made up of huge chunks of ice that push against each other, noisily creating a chaos of steep, broken slabs and dangerous crevasses. In summer, huge chunks of ice break off from the icecaps and float out to sea as icebergs.

Life among the ice

Despite the bitter cold and ice, the polar regions have a surprising amount of wildlife. Living on the landmasses around the edges of the Arctic Ocean there are large herds of reindeer or caribou, as well as musk oxen, Arctic wolves, foxes and hares whose white fur provides winter camouflage in the snow. The most famous dweller in the Arctic is the polar bear, which roams far and wide among the ice floes, feeding off its main prey, seals. There are also numerous birds, such as snowy owls, snow geese, Arctic skuas and the Arctic tern.

There is virtually no wildlife in the middle of the Antarctic continent, but many animals live along its coasts and in the surrounding seas, which are rich in fish. Many different kinds of penguin live on the shores of the Antarctic coast, and further north on the islands surrounding the Antarctic. The largest of these is the emperor penguin. The various kinds of seal include the large leopard seal, which, like the killer whale, is an aggressive hunter of penguins.

Shaggy musk oxen huddle together in herds for warmth and protection. They do not migrate at the onset of winter, but remain in the far north eating moss and lichen which they scrape up from beneath the snow.

The leopard seal often catches penguins for its food.

Eskimos and Inuit

Whereas no people have ever settled permanently within the Antarctic Circle, the ancestors of the Eskimo people have inhabited the far north for thousands of years. The name Inuit (singular: Inuk) is preferred by these people to Eskimo, which comes from an American Indian word meaning 'eaters of raw flesh'.

All the Eskimo peoples were experts at surviving the harsh conditions of the polar regions. They knew how to dress to keep out the cold, what food to eat, how to travel with dogs and sledges, and how to read the weather and the conditions of the treacherous ice. Many of the early polar explorers ignored the tried and tested ways of survival of the Eskimos but Peary and Amundsen learned as much as they could from the long experience of the Eskimos, and adapted this knowledge to their own aims.

Exotic spices became very popular in Europe in the 15th century. The first polar explorers were actually looking for new trade routes to the far east, in order to satisfy the demand for luxury goods such as silk and spices.

European explorers

The first European explorers in the polar regions came in search of sea routes to the Far East. Silk, spices and gems from the Far East had been traded by land across Asia to Europe even in Roman times. But, until the 15th century, Europeans were only vaguely aware that these exotic goods came from rich civilisations in eastern and southern Asia, such as China and India. Marco Polo spent many years in China between 1271 and 1295, but on his return to Europe few people believed his amazing tales.

The 15th century was the beginning of an age of great European sea voyages which started with the Portuguese exploration of the West African coast.

The Spanish and the Portuguese had soon established control of new sea routes to the East. These hugely valuable trade routes led around the southernmost tips of Africa and South America. However, the Dutch, English and French also wanted to find their own routes, and they began to look for a way to the East around the northernmost lands of the world.

The Northeast Passage

One idea was to sail eastwards, beyond the northern shores of Scandinavia. The Dutch navigator Willem Barents made three expeditions in this direction during the 1590s, but on each

While searching for the Northeast Passage, Barents' expedition became trapped in the ice. Barents died in his attempt to return to Holland.

occasion he found the route blocked by ice. On his last expedition in 1596–7, Barents' ship was trapped by ice off the island of Novaya Zemlya, north of Russia, and he and his crew were forced to spend the winter there. They built a hut out of driftwood and survived by hunting. The following spring they set off in two small boats to try to reach Holland. Barents himself died on the way, but 12 out of the 16 crew lived to tell the tale.

We now know that there is a sea route passing north of Russia to the Bering Strait, but it is almost always blocked by ice. It was not until 1878–9 that anyone managed to sail along this route, and only since the 1930s, after the invention of powerful icebreakers, has the Northeast Passage been in regular use.

The Northwest Passage

After Columbus had reached America in 1492, various European expeditions explored the east coast of North America, and later sailed up the west coast. Was there a sea route across the top of this continent?

In 1576 the English navigator, Martin Frobisher, made his first attempt to sail between the islands of northeastern Canada in search of such a route. He reached Frobisher Bay, on what is now called Baffin Island, before turning back, believing that the way through the Northwest Passage lay ahead.

Henry Hudson, his son and loyal crew members were cast adrift in Hudson Bay in 1611.

The terrible hardships facing crews in these waters are illustrated by the tragic tale of Henry Hudson, another English navigator. He was hired by a trading company to find a northern passage to the Far East. In 1610, taking his young son John with him, he sailed through what is now called the Hudson Strait into Hudson Bay. This is a huge area of water in northern Canada — so huge that Hudson believed he had found the Pacific Ocean. He sailed to the very south of the bay, into James Bay, where the onset of winter forced him to stop. In the spring Hudson wanted to push west in the hope of finding a passage out of the bay. But the crew, now exhausted, hungry and sick, had had enough. Most of the crewmen mutinied, accusing Hudson of hiding away food

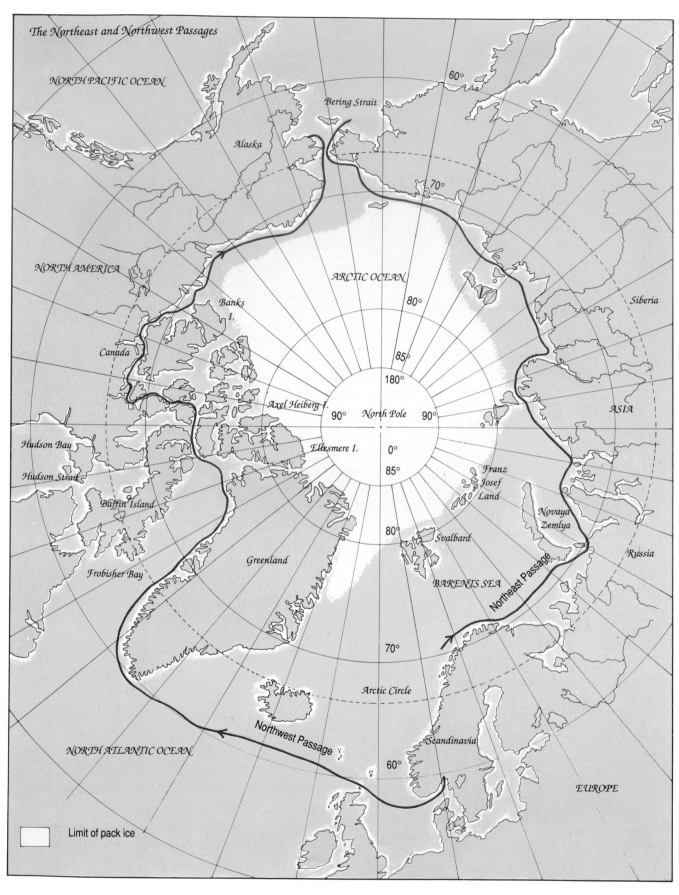

The Northeast and Northwest Passages

NORTH PACIFIC OCEAN

60°

Bering Strait

Alaska

70°

NORTH AMERICA

ARCTIC OCEAN

Siberia

Banks I.

80°

85°

180°

Canada

Axel Heiberg I.

90° North Pole 90°

ASIA

Ellesmere I.

0°

Hudson Bay

85°

Franz Josef Land

Hudson Strait

Novaya Zemlya

Baffin Island

80°

Svalbard

Russia

Greenland

BARENTS SEA

Northeast Passage

Frobisher Bay

70°

Northwest Passage

NORTH ATLANTIC OCEAN

Arctic Circle

60°

Scandinavia

EUROPE

Limit of pack ice

for himself. They put him, his son and a few loyal crewmen in a boat and cast them adrift, then returned to England. Nothing was ever heard of Hudson again.

In the history of polar exploration — both Arctic and Antarctic — wildlife became an early victim. After earlier expeditions Hudson had taken reports back about the large numbers of whales that he had seen. As as result, the whaling industry expanded rapidly. By 1700, hundreds of European whaling ships were operating in the cold waters of the North Atlantic.

More names for the map

If there was a Northwest Passage, it clearly lay further north than Hudson Bay. But this elusive route continued to defeat navigators for nearly three centuries. After John Franklin's expedition came to grief in 1847 (see box), it seemed an impossible goal. However, one of the many expeditions that took part in the search for Franklin did, in fact, prove the existence of the Northwest Passage. The expedition, led by Robert McClure, sailed through the Bering Strait and headed eastwards. But McClure's ship became stuck in the ice off Banks Island and the explorers were eventually themselves rescued by a sledging party who were also looking for Franklin. They were then taken home

The Franklin expedition

At the time, no journey of exploration attracted more attention than the British naval expedition led by Sir John Franklin, which left Britain in 1845. Franklin was in charge of 137 men on board two ships, HMS *Erebus* and HMS *Terror*. Franklin appeared to have every chance of achieving the expedition's goal: the conquest of the Northwest Passage.

By 1848, when no news of the expedition had been heard, it was clear that something had gone terribly wrong. Rescue expeditions were mounted one after the other — 40 in all. Bit by bit the story of the expedition was revealed. In 1854, a Scottish explorer was told by some Inuit that they had seen a large party of starving Europeans struggling with a sledge some years previously. Another expedition set out in 1857, sponsored by Franklin's wife. This expedition came across messages on King William Island which told of Franklin's death in 1847. He had died of scurvy, a disease caused by lack of the vitamin C which is found in fresh food. According to these messages the 105 survivors, who had suffered three Arctic winters trapped in the ice, now intended to head overland in a bid to reach civilisation. Since then the scattered remains of the expedition members have been found where each had died of cold and illness. Four bodies were found as late as September 1994.

The *Erebus* and the *Terror* seen in the background of an imaginary polar landscape. Franklin's expedition aroused great curiosity at home, and inspired some fanciful illustrations such as this one.

Little was known about the southern regions of the world in 1670, when this map was drawn.

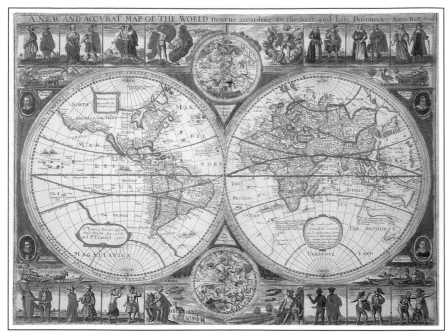

Amundsen's tiny ship, the *Gjøa*, was the first to sail right through the Northwest Passage, in 1903–6.

eastwards in 1854. McClure and his men therefore became the first men to complete the Northwest Passage, but it was 50 years before a boat succeeded in passing through it from one end to the other. In 1903–6, a small ship called *Gjøa* sailed to the north of Baffin Island, then west, wintering among the Inuit before eventually continuing its journey to the Bering Strait. The leader of the *Gjøa* expedition was a young Norwegian. His name was Roald Amundsen

The Magnetic Poles

The North and South Poles are situated at the point where all the lines of longitude meet at the top and bottom of the globe. They are known as the Geographic Poles.

However, a magnetic compass points to the Magnetic North Pole. This is because the earth has a magnetic field which, like an ordinary magnet, has north and south poles along which its magnetism lines up. The Magnetic North Pole is not the same as the Geographic North Pole: in fact it drifts slowly around as a result of the effects of the earth's orbit on the magnetism in the earth's core. Today the Magnetic North Pole lies about 1000 kilometres from the Geographic North Pole, in northern Canada. The Magnetic South Pole is positioned just off the Antarctic coast south of Australia.

The unknown southern continent

While the rest of the world was being explored, mapped and large areas claimed by the Europeans during the 16th and 17th centuries, maps of the world still marked a huge, vague continent in the south called *Terra Australis Incognita*, the 'Unknown Southern Land'. The Dutch knew about Australia, and the Dutch explorer Abel Tasman sailed around the continent in 1642–4. But it was not until over 100 years later, in 1770, that Captain Cook explored the east coast of Australia and claimed it for Britain.

What was this *Terra Australis Incognita*? Was there any major area of land to the south of Australia? This was the question that Cook's second expedition (1772–5) set out to answer. In his ship, the *Resolution*, Cook sailed right around the world, venturing as far south as he dared and crossing the Antarctic Circle twice. He found nothing but ice, and concluded that there was indeed no habitable landmass south of Australia. Captain Cook was one of the first of a new kind of explorer who travelled mainly in the interests of

Large numbers of fur seals used to inhabit the islands around Antarctica, but they were almost wiped out by seal hunters in the 1820s.

science and geography. He and his crew made careful observations and records about the places they visited. As a result, maps of these areas became more accurate and reliable, and no longer showed *Terra Australis Incognita*. They did, however, show the islands of South Georgia, where Cook reported an immense wealth of fur seals and other wildlife.

Sadly, it was this observation that was to have the greatest impact on the next stage of Antarctic exploration. After Cook's reports became known, European and North American seal hunters headed south and began the slaughter of thousands of fur seals for their valuable fur. Over 400,000 seals were killed in three years in one group of Antarctic islands, virtually wiping out the species. The hunters then concentrated on the cumbersome elephant seal, whose blubber could be turned into useful oil.

During this period, the waters around South Georgia were visited by numerous ships, some of which ventured further south towards the Antarctic. They went mainly in search of seals and other prey, but some navigators made careful observations and records. One Russian navigator, Fabian Bellinghausen, led a scientific expedition which, like Cook's before him, circumnavigated the globe in the cold southern seas. In January 1820 Bellinghausen and others made a remarkable discovery: they saw land amongst the ice shelves of Antarctica. It provided the first inkling that there might be a southern continent after all.

Left alone for 50 years

Ship-based exploration of this ice-bound continent continued for another two decades. In 1839–43, a British expedition led by Sir James Clark Ross travelled to Antarctica in two ships, the *Erebus* and the *Terror* — used again in 1845 by Franklin's ill-fated Arctic expedition. In the area south of Australia the expedition discovered Ross Island and its active volcano, now named Mount Erebus, as well as the Ross Ice Shelf, a huge area of ice the size of France which is fronted by an ice cliff 70 metres high. The Ross Ice Shelf was to become the starting point for the overland Antarctic expeditions in the race to reach the South Pole. But that was not for another 50 years: in the meantime there was little further exploration of this newly discovered, hostile continent.

Horizons

You could find out about these explorers who all played a part in the early exploration of the Arctic and Antarctica: John Davis (English explorer after whom the Davis Strait between Greenland and Baffin Island is named); Charles Wilkes (led US Navy expedition which discovered more areas of the Antarctic continent); James Weddell (British navigator who gave his name to the Weddell Sea in Antarctica); Jules Dumont d'Urville (French explorer who discovered Terre Adélie in Antarctica).

Transport and equipment

Brave first attempts

During the 19th century, the attention of Arctic explorers gradually shifted away from the Northwest Passage to the idea of reaching the North Pole itself. It was fairly clear that to reach the Pole, explorers would have to cross the ice — although some theories suggested that there might be a large, unfrozen sea in the middle.

The British firmly believed in manhauling — pulling sledges without the assistance of dogs.

Such overland expeditions required careful planning, since all the food and other equipment needed had to be prepared and packed, and then hauled over the ice. British expeditions believed that the hard physical labour of a human team struggling together to pull their sledges loaded with equipment in very difficult circumstances, known as manhauling, gave the explorers the will to survive and to succeed. But this approach would eventually cause Britain to lose the race to both Poles.

Huskies

In contrast to the British tradition of manhauling, both Peary and Amundsen were convinced that the form of transport used by the Eskimos, husky dogs, provided the best means of moving across the ice. Huskies are a breed of extremely tough, half-tame dogs. They originally come from Siberia, but are used all around the Arctic Circle. Huskies are specially adapted to the freezing climate with thick, oily fur which keeps out the cold so effectively that they can sleep outdoors for much of the year. A team of six or more dogs, hitched to a sledge by harnesses and traces, can pull

Huskies are well-protected from the cold by their thick, oily fur.

Huskies usually work in teams of between six and 12 dogs, each attached to the sledge by a trace.

heavy loads up to 80 kilometres per day. The dogs can reach speeds of over 30 kilometres per hour, and can be driven for 18 hours at a stretch. All that they demand is that they are kept well-fed: seal meat is their usual diet.

Huskies are working dogs, not pets. Helmer Hanssen, Amundsen's most experienced dog-handler wrote: 'For us humans driving to the South Pole was just like play, but it was no fun for the dogs. They had to be driven hard and whipped if we were ever to get there…' In fact, it was worse than this. Huskies are happy to eat dog meat. As Amundsen neared the Pole, his party no longer needed all the dogs. Twenty-four huskies were shot to provide meat for the others. It may seem cruel, but Amundsen had learned this technique of survival from the Eskimos, and he accepted it as a necessary evil.

Clothing and food

Peary and Amundsen also learned important lessons from the Eskimos about the kinds of clothing and food that were suitable for polar exploration. Many early European explorers in the Arctic insisted on wearing their own style of clothes, such as leather boots, woollen shirts, felt jackets and fur coats. The Eskimo people did not have any other materials besides skin and fur, but these proved to be the best for the extreme climate of the far north.

In winter, Eskimos wore at least two layers of clothing. These two layers trapped air in-between, and air is one of the most effective forms of insulation. The inner layer was made of soft fur or bird feathers, and consisted of a tunic with a hood, trousers and socks, with the fur turned inwards for extra warmth.

Many British expeditions to the polar regions wore European-made clothes (right) which were twice as heavy as Eskimo fur clothing (below).

The outer layer, with fur turned outwards, was a pair of trousers tucked into high fur boots, mittens, and another tunic with a hood. The sleeves were wide enough for the wearer to pull his or her arms inside for warmth. The hood was lined with wolverine or wolf fur, because this fur reduces the problem of condensed breath settling and turning to ice.

A complete outfit of Eskimo clothing weighed about five kilograms: European polar clothing weighed at least twice as much. In places where you need to conserve as much energy as possible to survive, such factors were vital.

The cook making pies at Scott's base camp in 1911 (see page 32). At base camp, expeditions tried to make life as comfortable as possible.

The cooking range in the hut used by Shackleton on his 1914 Antarctic expedition (see page 40).

One of the most essential features for any polar expedition is the careful planning of food supplies. Since all food — for humans as well as for dogs — has to be carried by an expedition, the quantities have to be calculated with great precision. The food has to be nutritious and well-balanced. If humans do not eat enough vitamin C (found naturally in fruit, vegetables and fresh meat) they will get scurvy, a painful disease that can result in death. Scurvy can be avoided in warmer parts of the world by including fresh fruit, such as limes, in the diet, but limes quickly lose their effectiveness in polar conditions. Amundsen had a particular interest in scurvy because he had suffered from the disease on a previous expedition. He noticed that Eskimos avoid scurvy by eating seal meat, and so he included quantities of this meat in his food supplies.

Amundsen's other stand-by was pemmican. This is a form of dried meat prepared by native North Americans. Amundsen developed similar preparations using meat and fish, adding vegetables and oatmeal. The result was a highly nutritious food that could be eaten raw or cooked. Portions were carefully measured out in advance and moulded into blocks to last one man for one day.

Other foods taken on Amundsen's sledges included biscuits, dried milk and chocolate, while at base camp the expedition could enjoy all kinds of luxuries, such as tinned meat and vegetables, bacon, cheese, caramel puddings and wine.

Bomb vessels

Ships played an important part in both Peary's and Amundsen's polar explorations, as the form of transport by which they reached their respective base camps.

A polar region is no place for an ordinary ship. Ice packed around the hull exerts an enormous force, which can not only trap a ship but crush it. Naval expeditions in the early 19th century met the problem by using 'bomb vessels' — ships that had specially thick, reinforced hulls, designed to withstand the massive force of cannons as they were fired on deck. Ross's ships *Erebus* and *Terror* (see page 11) were both bomb vessels.

The first ever ship to be purpose-built for polar regions was the *Fram* belonging to the famous Norwegian explorer, Fridtjof Nansen. The *Fram* was a broad vessel, 36 metres long and 10 metres wide, built to withstand the pressure of being lodged in the ice. Its rounded hull was shaped so that when the ice pressed against it the whole ship would lift up and so avoid being crushed. Other special features included insulation to keep the cold out and the heat in, and ventilation to allow the air to circulate in order to prevent condensation and dampness — a notorious problem in ships in cold conditions.

At its launch in 1892, the *Fram* was officially given its name, which means 'Forward'. The *Fram*'s first expedition lasted three years, during which the ship drifted in the ice to the south of the North Pole (see page 18).

In 1907, Nansen agreed to let Amundsen use the *Fram* on his next expedition. Amundsen was delighted to have the use of such a ship. With his typical thoroughness, Amundsen proceeded to make alterations to the *Fram*, giving her triangular sails at the back and front to make her easier to handle. He also replaced the steam engine with a newly invented diesel one, which the crew christened 'Old Whooping Cough'. The *Fram*'s only drawback was that it had a peculiar motion at sea which tended to make passengers seasick. It was, nonetheless, a ship perfectly suited for its purpose — a 'Viking ship in the 20th century', as another explorer described it.

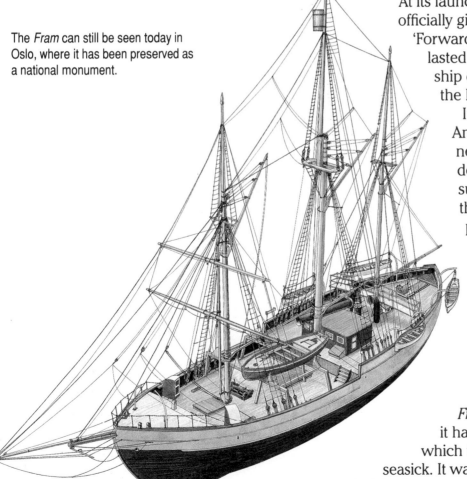

The *Fram* can still be seen today in Oslo, where it has been preserved as a national monument.

To the North Pole

Fridtjof Nansen

After his first sea voyage in the Arctic aged 22 (in 1882) the Norwegian scientist Fridtjof Nansen set his heart on a career of polar exploration. In 1888, he led a team of six men to complete the first overland crossing of Greenland. What was notable about this journey was the way that he adapted his knowledge of Lapp (see page 39) and Inuit ways of travel to achieve his aims. On his famous *Fram* expedition of 1893–6, he used dog sledges and Inuit kayaks. In fact, this was his last major expedition, but by this time he had become the hero of a new breed of polar explorers, notably his fellow Norwegian, Roald Amundsen.

Fridtjof Nansen, one of the great heroes of Arctic exploration

The First International Polar Year

About 15 polar expeditions took place in 1882–3. This was the First International Polar Year. The intention of the Polar Year was not to attempt to reach the Poles, but rather to assemble as much information as possible about both polar regions — their weather, geography and other observations — which would then be put at the disposal of all scientists and explorers.

One of these expeditions took a tragic course when only seven out of a group of 26 men returned after an unsuccessful attempt to reach the North Pole. But nevertheless much good work was done. Furthermore, it allowed a new kind of explorer to emerge — the scientist who could use the accumulated wisdom of other expeditions to discover the best ways to survive and travel in polar conditions in order to carry out projects as safely and efficiently as possible.

Exploring in the *Fram*

One of the greatest polar explorers to emerge during this period was the Norwegian, Fridtjof Nansen. In the early 1890s he laid the plans for an unusual expedition. His specially reinforced ship, the *Fram* (see page 17), would be allowed to become stuck in the ice to the north of Russia to see if the ocean drift would carry it close to the North Pole. This idea had evolved as a result of an earlier expedition in which a ship had become trapped in the ice in the Bering Strait. Remnants from the wrecked ship had later been found on the southwest coast of Greenland. This pointed to the existence of an ocean drift across the Arctic, and this is what Nansen now set out to examine.

Nansen and the *Fram*, under the command of Otto Sverdrup, left Norway in June 1893 and spent three years in the ice. By March 1895 it was clear that the drift of the ice would take them to the south of the North Pole, so Nansen and a companion, Hjalmar Johansen, set off with kayaks and dog sledges and enough food for 100 days. They came to within 360 kilometres of the Pole, the nearest to date, but then the ice started to break up and drift southwards, so they turned back.

By now they had lost touch with the *Fram* and were forced to spend the winter on Franz Josef Land, one of a large group of islands to the north of Russia. In the spring, Nansen returned to Norway — arriving home just before the *Fram*, which had eventually broken free of the ice after a journey of 35 months. It had been an epic voyage, which had not only proved the drift of the ice, but also provided valuable evidence that the Arctic was indeed an ocean.

Nansen and his companion Johansen leave the *Fram* and set off across the polar ice.

Training in Greenland

In the same years that Nansen was travelling in Greenland and through the Arctic ice on the *Fram*, a very determined American was exploring similar territory. Robert Peary was born in 1856 in Pennsylvania, USA. As a child he was a keen naturalist and walker, and he was always highly ambitious. He became an engineer in the US Navy and spent some time in Nicaragua, Central America, surveying the site of a proposed canal. Peary treated this task as if he was exploring new territory, but his first real expedition was to Greenland in 1886. He led two further expeditions to northern Greenland (to an area now called Peary Land) in 1891–2 and 1893–5, establishing for the first time that Greenland is an island. Peary married in 1888, and his wife, Josephine, accompanied him on the 1893–5 expedition, giving birth to their first daughter in Greenland. She was called Marie Ahnighito (meaning 'snow baby') Peary.

What was different about Peary when compared to earlier Arctic explorers was his approach to polar travel. He befriended the Greenland Inuit, used their help wherever possible, and adopted as many of their techniques of travel and survival as he needed to meet his aims. He used dogs and sledges, he dressed in Inuit clothes, and he was prepared to eat Inuit food. After his last Greenland expedition, he became determined to be the first person at the North Pole. This determination was close to an obsession.

Peary believed strongly that huskies were the key to success in polar travel. He is seen here with one of the 246 dogs which accompanied him from Greenland aboard the *Roosevelt*.

Losing his toes

Peary made his first attempt to reach the Pole in 1898, and tried again in 1899, each time using Fort Conger, on Ellesmere Island, as his base. At

Frostbite

In very cold conditions, parts of the human body can literally become frozen. This usually happens first of all to the body's extremities — the fingers, toes, cheeks, earlobes and nose. It is not actually painful because the cold numbs the nerves in the affected parts. But frostbite stops the circulation of blood, and the affected areas of the body begin to die. If it is not severe, frostbite can be treated by gentle warmth — this is when it can become extremely painful. However, in bad cases the dead parts may become infected and eventually poison the whole body. In such circumstances, the only treatment may be amputation.

Robert Bartlett (right), the captain of the *Roosevelt*, accompanied Peary and his team to a point 222 kilometres from the North Pole.

this time he was convinced that he was in competition with the Norwegian, Otto Sverdrup, who had commanded the *Fram* on Nansen's 1893–6 expedition. As a result, he pushed himself to the limits, travelling in midwinter darkness in temperatures as low as -52°C. When Peary returned to Fort Conger in 1899, Matthew Henson — his black companion who took part in all of his expeditions — peeled off Peary's boots to discover that most of Peary's toes were so frostbitten that they came off as well. The loss of eight toes made it difficult for Peary to walk for any great distance, but this did not lessen his determination to reach the North Pole. 'There is no time to pamper sick men on the trail,' he wrote. 'A few toes were not much to give to achieve the Pole.'

Preparing for the Pole

Peary led more expeditions in 1902 and 1906, gradually pressing further and further north. In 1908, now aged 52, he began another attempt to reach the North Pole. This time he was determined to succeed, and planned the journey meticulously.

Peary had made many useful contacts and friends among the Inuit of northern Greenland. He intended to use their skills to the full. The plan was to send groups forward with supplies to prepare a series of relay stations. The main party would then speed along in their tracks, saving their energies for the final leg, the journey to the Pole itself. 'My theory was to work the supporting parties to the limit in order to keep the main party fresh,' he wrote.

In July 1908, Peary left New York for Ellesmere Island on a ship called the *Roosevelt*, with five other Americans, including Matthew Henson, who would take part in the attempt on the Pole. On the way, the *Roosevelt* also picked up 49 Inuit men, women and children and 246 dogs.

After spending the winter aboard the *Roosevelt*, the expedition set off on 1 March 1909. It was still winter in the Arctic, but Peary preferred the firm ice conditions at this time of year, even if the hours of daylight were short and the cold was intense. It was tough going: the ice was a chaos of frosted ridges, some over 20 metres high. Every now and then the surface would split open revealing a channel of water which would delay progress until it closed up again, or until the expedition either managed to cross it on an ice raft or make a time-consuming

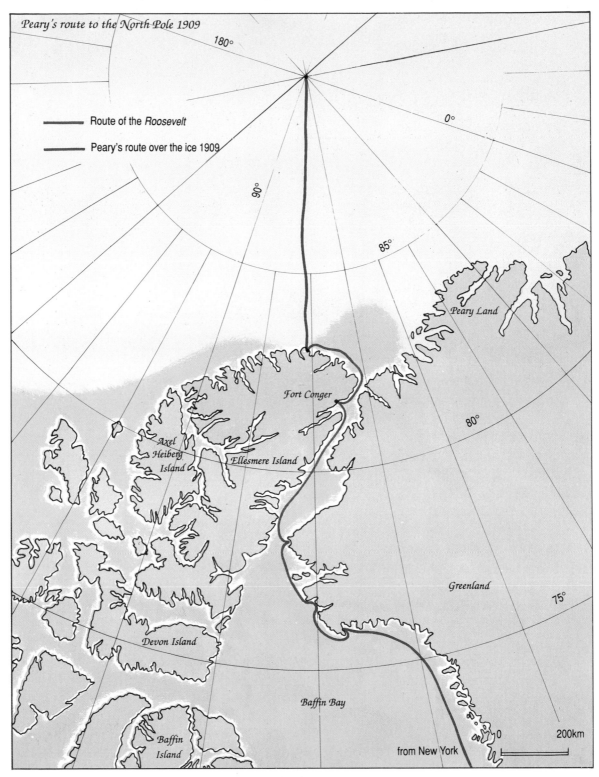

Peary's route to the North Pole 1909

——— Route of the *Roosevelt*

——— Peary's route over the ice 1909

180°

0°

90°

85°

Peary Land

Fort Conger

80°

Axel
Heiberg
Island

Ellesmere Island

Greenland

75°

Devon Island

Baffin Bay

0   200km

Baffin
Island

from New York

detour. Peary travelled on a sledge for most of the way, as the loss of his toes prevented him from going far by foot. At night the expedition slept in igloos prepared by the Inuit.

By 1 April the main party had reached the final supply station. All that remained were five 40-kilometre marches to be undertaken by Peary himself, Matthew Henson and four Inuit: Ukkujaak, Oodaaq, Iggianguaq and Silluk. On 6 April Peary's diary entry reads: 'The Pole at last!!! The prize of 3 centuries, my dream & ambition for 23 years. *Mine* at last.'

High ridges of ice proved to be exhausting obstacles, and slowed down Peary's progress to the Pole.

Polar navigation

Knowing where you are in the polar regions presents problems. It is possible to navigate by observing the position of the sun and stars and by measuring their angles with a sextant. A compass can be used, but the direction in which a compass needle points becomes increasingly unreliable as you get closer to the Magnetic Poles. A tracking wheel attached to a sledge will give a rough idea of the distance travelled.

However, the extreme cold makes it difficult to use any instruments, the sun is frequently obscured by cloud or blizzards, and there are few landmarks to go by. It is easy for polar explorers to stray off their path and even to go round in circles. Of course, there were no physical features on the surface of the earth to mark the Poles, so anyone claiming to reach the Poles had to make very careful observations to be sure they had indeed arrived at 90° of latitude.

They built an igloo at the Pole, and Peary slept for three hours. They stayed for a further 30 hours, taking bearings and photos, before starting for home. Their return journey was astonishingly quick: they covered 780 kilometres in just 19 days, reaching the *Roosevelt* in triumph on 25 April.

They had to wait until summer before the *Roosevelt* could get free of the ice. Peary returned to the USA in late September, having already lodged his claim to have been the first to reach the North Pole. To his horror, however, he was not given the reception he had expected.

A counter-claim

Peary reported the news of his success in *The New York Times* on 9 September 1909. But six days beforehand another American explorer had announced that he had reached the Pole on 21 April 1908 — a year before Peary. The name of this explorer was Frederick Cook, and he had been the doctor on Peary's 1891–2 expedition to the north of Greenland.

Cook claimed that he had travelled with two Inuit and 26 dogs from Axel Heiberg Island in the north of Canada. His return journey had taken him over a year, and eventually he had reached Denmark where the news was announced. It seemed clear that he had made an epic journey, but had he reached the Pole? Many people believed Cook, and remained convinced that he was the first man to reach the North Pole.

Peary's triumph had been badly upstaged, and he was furious. He declared Cook a liar, and spent the last 11 years of his life

The dispute between Peary and Cook: headlines from *The New York Times* 9 September 1909

Horizons

You could find out about these other Arctic explorers: George Washington de Long (led tragic expedition to the Arctic in 1879); Adolphus Greeley (survived near-starvation in the Arctic by eating seaweed, lichen and the expedition's leather sleeping bags); Vilhjalmur Stefansson (lived among the Inuit and travelled extensively in the Arctic); Mylius Erichsen (polar explorer whose northern Greenland expedition of 1907 showed Peary's maps to be inaccurate); Alfred Wegener (formed the theory of continental drift).

fighting to have his achievement recognised. In a series of hearings, the accounts of Peary and Cook were studied in depth by the US Congress — a process which, according to his wife, left Peary depressed and bitter. In 1911, Congress decided in favour of Peary.

Peary was by then generally acknowledged to be the first man to have reached the North Pole. However, Cook's story was not entirely discredited, and Cook's name was still mentioned in the same breath as Peary's, casting a shadow over Peary's achievement. Even at his death in 1940, many people believed that Cook had reached the Pole first, and some people still do. Some of his observations that were rejected at the time have since proved to be accurate.

More recently, serious doubts have been raised about Peary's journey — not just whether he was the first man to reach the Pole, but whether he had in fact reached the Pole at all. The speed of his journey, especially the return journey, led to doubts that he could have travelled such a long distance in the time. More damaging was the fact that Peary had written his diary entry for 6 April, the day he claimed to have reached the Pole, on a separate sheet of paper. In fact, at this point in the diary itself there were four blank pages. Had Peary written the entry after the event? Had Peary's obsessive ambition and determination not to fail caused him to bend the truth? Today Peary's claim still remains in dispute, and he may not have been the first man to reach the North Pole after all.

To the South Pole

On land in the Antarctic

The Antarctic had been virtually forgotten in the last 50 years of the 19th century, but interest in this mysterious continent reawakened in the 1890s. A Norwegian called Carsten Borchgrevinck made the briefest of journeys in Antarctica — just two hours — in 1895. Borchgrevinck was determined to return to this hostile land, and eventually found British sponsors who mounted the 'British Antarctic Expedition'. In 1899 a ship delivered Borchgrevinck and nine others, plus 75 dogs, to a base camp at Cape Adare, on the north-western edge of the Ross Sea. They stayed there throughout the polar winter before being picked up again in January 1900. The achievement was modest, but they had been further south that anyone before them, and they were the first people to spend the winter on the Antarctic continent.

Scott's first expedition

At the same time, in Britain another major Antarctic expedition was being organised, and to some extent Borgrevinck's achievements were considered an unwelcome distraction from it. Called the British National Antarctic Expedition, it was led by Captain Robert Falcon Scott. Arriving in Antarctica aboard the *Discovery* in 1901, Scott made his base camp in McMurdo Sound, to the west of the Ross Ice Shelf. The main aim of the

Hut Point, at McMurdo Sound, was the starting point for Scott's 1901–4 expedition. This watercolour was painted by Edward Wilson.

expedition was scientific research, but Scott also wanted to make an attempt on the Pole. In 1902 Scott, accompanied by Dr Edward ('Bill') Wilson and Ernest Shackleton, crossed much of the Ross Ice Shelf, reaching the furthest south yet. It was a desperate journey lasting 93 days, during which the three men faced terrible weather, nearly ran out of supplies, and began to suffer from scurvy. They had taken 19 dogs with them, dragging five sledges, but the dogs proved unsuccessful and either died or were shot. In fact, they were simply not being properly cared for and fed, but it was enough to convince Scott that dogs were not the best means of travel in the Antarctic. In future he would depend on manhauling (see page 14) and ponies. This was to be a fatal mistake. Nonetheless, the *Discovery* returned home in triumph in 1904 and Scott was acclaimed as the most experienced Antarctic explorer of his day.

Ernest Shackleton

Scott had now decided that his goal was to reach the South Pole, but it was Ernest Shackleton who had the first opportunity to achieve this. After the journey of 1902 Shackleton had fallen out with Scott, irritated by his style of leadership. Nevertheless, Shackleton agreed with Scott that manhauling was the way to travel. In 1908, he returned to the Antarctic and set out for the Pole with three other men and four ponies. The expedition crossed the Ross Ice Shelf, climbed 3000 metres up the Beardmore Glacier and came to within 180 kilometres of the Pole. Exhausted and running out of supplies, Shackleton knew they could not make it. They turned back. After coming so far, and being so near their goal, it was a courageous decision. But as Shackleton put it, 'better to be a live donkey than a dead lion.'

The route to the South Pole lay beyond the glaciers and mountains that border the Ross Ice Shelf.

The race is on

The way was open for Scott. His second Antarctic expedition set off from London in June 1910, on board the *Terra Nova*. Scott had two aims: to continue his scientific research, and to plant the British flag on the South Pole. This second aim had become all the more urgent since the North Pole had been claimed by Peary and Cook the previous year. 'What matters now,' Scott wrote, 'is that the Pole should be attained by an Englishman.' Scott was confident that this goal lay within his reach. But there was a shock in store for him. When he stopped in Australia on the way south he received a telegram: 'Beg leave to inform you *Fram* proceeding Antarctic. Amundsen.'

Secret mission

'To the explorer,' wrote Roald Amundsen, 'adventure is merely an unwelcome interruption of his serious labours… An adventure is merely a bit of bad planning, brought to light by the test of trial.' Bad planning was not a fault that Amundsen suffered from. Like the best polar explorers he did everything to reduce risk by studying the most efficient and effective ways of travel and survival, by planning and calculating everything down to the last detail, and by leaving as little as possible to chance.

It is perhaps surprising, therefore, that when Amundsen was planning his 1910 expedition he was not intending to go to the South Pole at all. By this time he was a famous and respected Arctic explorer. Born near Oslo in 1872, at the age of 15 Amundsen was so inspired by the accounts of Franklin's explorations that he decided he too wanted to be an Arctic explorer. At his mother's insistence Amundsen studied medicine for two years, but when she died he gave up his studies to pursue his chosen career. In 1887–9 he took part in a Belgian expedition to the Antarctic on board a ship called the *Belgica*. The *Belgica* became stuck in the ice and was the first ship to spend a winter in Antarctica. In 1903–6 Amundsen made his remarkable voyage in the *Gjøa* to become the first person to sail through the Northwest Passage (see page 12). During this journey he spent two winters with the Inuit, learning their ways and gaining a good understanding of how to handle dog teams.

In 1909, Amundsen's intention was to travel back to the Arctic aboard Nansen's *Fram*, and to make an attempt on the North Pole. But in September of that year, he received the news that Cook (who had been on the *Belgica* expedition as ship's doctor) and Peary both claimed to have reached the North Pole. Not only did this mean that Amundsen could no longer win this prize, he now also found it difficult to raise money for an expedition.

He decided instead to make a bid for the next great prize of polar exploration: the South Pole. It would be a personal triumph, but also a triumph for Norway, a nation which had become independent from Sweden as recently as 1905. He decided, however, to keep his decision a secret. He knew that

Amundsen in 1909, the year he was making plans to travel to the Arctic

The *Terra Nova*

Scott's expedition sailed in a ship called the *Terra Nova* ('New Land'). It was a handsome looking vessel, somewhat larger than the *Fram*. Unlike the *Fram*, however, it was not purpose-built for polar exploration.

The *Terra Nova* had several disadvantages. It had a steam engine, fuelled by coal, which required three men to feed it. It was also crowded, with 65 members of the expedition on board. Later, after the expedition had landed in Antarctica and set up its base camp, the *Terra Nova* started its journey to New Zealand, where it would spend winter. In the Bay of Whales it came across the *Fram*. The crew of the *Terra Nova* were invited on board the *Fram*. They were greatly impressed. Compared to their own ship, the *Fram* seemed positively luxurious. For his part, Thorvald Nilsen, second in command of the *Fram*, said of the *Terra Nova*, 'I must confess it did not look very inviting.'

It is true that the race for the South Pole was won and lost on the land, but the conditions on board the ships that brought the expeditions to Antarctica undoubtedly had an important effect on the mental and physical preparation of the expedition members.

Scott's ship, the *Terra Nova*

On board the *Terra Nova*. There were 65 crew members on Scott's ship, which made conditions on board extremely cramped.

Nansen hoped to take the *Fram* to the South Pole himself, and so, if he knew Amundsen's plans, would probably not allow him to use the ship.

When the *Fram* left Oslo on 7 June 1910 only two out of the ten expedition members knew its true destination: Kristian Prestrud, and Amundsen himself.

The *Terra Nova* came across the *Fram* in the Bay of Whales while Amundsen's expedition were still setting up Framheim.

Going south

At Madeira, in the Atlantic Ocean, Amundsen announced his change of plan. The other expedition members were shocked. Amundsen gave them the opportunity to return home, but they all agreed to continue.

On 11 January 1911, the *Fram* arrived in the Bay of Whales, at the eastern end of the Ross Ice Shelf, 1270 kilometres from the South Pole. The expedition quickly unloaded the 900 cases of stores and the dogs. Three kilometres from the edge of the Shelf, they put up a hut surrounded by tents as their base camp, which they called Framheim. The *Fram* then set off for Argentina, before the ice could close in around it.

In the six weeks of daylight before the onset of the polar winter, Amundsen and his party of eight busily set up a series of three storage depots at 100-kilometre intervals along the route that would take them to the Pole and back. These depots were carefully marked with numbered beacons so that they could be easily found. They contained food, sleeping bags, tents, clothes, cooking stoves, fuel and matches. The planning was meticulous, and the preparations all went smoothly. The expedition then returned to Framheim to sit out the winter.

Amundsen's base camp was established quickly after the expedition's arrival. The main building at Framheim was a prefabricated wooden hut.

Amundsen's team kept themselves busy in their quarters throughout the long polar winter by mending and improving their equipment.

Winter darkness and a false spring

The polar winter can be depressing. Nerves easily become frayed when you are cooped up in a hut with the same companions for six months. In the darkness it is hard to know if it is day or night, whether you should be awake or asleep, whether it is time for breakfast or dinner. These conditions call for a great deal of tolerance, and self-discipline. Amundsen's team managed admirably. They busied themselves by preparing for their journey and improving their equipment, for example by reducing the weight of their heavy sledges by cutting and planing the wood. The cook, Adolf Lindstrøm, kept the team in good humour by producing magnificent meals from the food in his storerooms, which he had tunnelled into the ice.

By August, with the arrival of the first sunlight at the end of the Antarctic winter, they were ready and impatient to go. So, when the temperature at last rose in early September, Amundsen decided to begin the quest for the Pole. However, Hjalmar Johansen, Nansen's highly experienced companion from the 1893–6 *Fram* expedition, warned against it: it was a false spring, he said, and the weather would soon turn cold again.

Amundsen chose to ignore this warning, but Johansen was right. The expedition set out on 8 September. On 12 September, the temperature dropped to -53°C. The dogs were suffering and they made little progress. Amundsen decided to turn back, and the party, frostbitten and depressed, returned to Framheim after just seven days. Worse, Johansen criticised Amundsen for heading back to camp in advance of the rest of the party. Relationships suddenly became fraught.

Off at last

Eventually the weather improved, and on 20 October Amundsen set off again. He travelled with four others: Olav Bjaaland, Sverre Hassel, Oscar Wisting, and Helmer Hanssen. Johansen was left behind to join Kristian Prestrud on a separate scientific expedition. Johansen accepted Amundsen's decision, but he was bitterly disappointed. For Amundsen, however, it was a clear choice. He believed in decisive leadership, and Johansen had made the serious error of criticising him.

Despite the fact that they had 48 dogs for four sledges, the party made slow progress in poor conditions, negotiating crevasses in visibility reduced by continuous snow. But by 12 November they had passed all their supply depots and reached the beginning of the 3000-metre climb to the plateau on which the South Pole sits. On 17 November they began to go up the dangerous, jagged slopes of the Axel Heiberg Glacier (named after a Norwegian who

Much of the South Polar icecap is covered by a thick crust of ice and snow, packed into bumpy ridges by the vicious winds that blow across the continent.

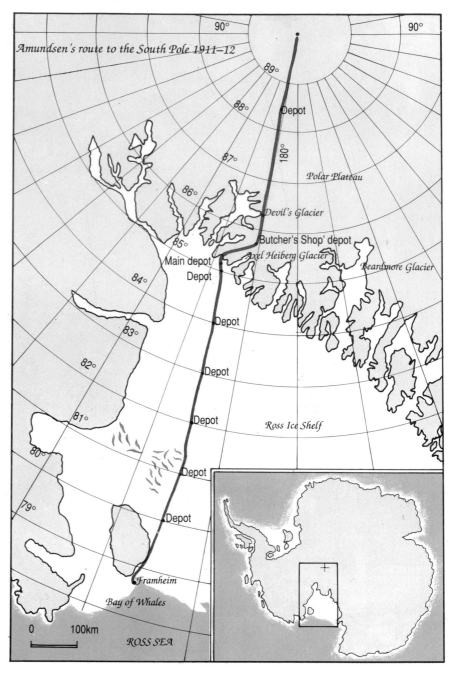

sponsored polar exploration). This was uncharted territory.
Shackleton had approached the Pole from the other side of the
Ross Ice Shelf, climbing the Beardmore Glacier. The dogs
performed magnificently, and they succeeded in reaching the top
of the glacier in four days.

The Butcher's Shop

They had now come to a place which, in Amundsen's plan of the
journey, he had labelled 'The Butcher's Shop'. Here 24 of the
weakest dogs were shot, leaving three teams of six pulling three
sledges. Shooting the dogs was a hateful task which no-one
enjoyed, least of all Hanssen who had to shoot a dog that had
accompanied him on earlier expeditions to the Arctic. But every-
one agreed that this was essential to the success of their mission.

Suddenly the weather turned bad, and the party were pinned to their camp at The Butcher's Shop for four days, unable to advance. In the end they decided to push on, despite the weather, making difficult progress for the next two weeks.

They climbed an awkward glacier, pitted with crevasses, which they christened Devil's Glacier, and on 4 December they at last reached the final plateau. Progress had been slow, but things were going to plan. After four more days of poor weather, they reached 88° 23' south — the point where Shackleton had turned back two years previously. Amundsen was by now deeply impressed by Shackleton's record, which had been achieved by human energy alone.

The South Pole

Suddenly the weather improved, and Amundsen's team, their goal in sight, sped southwards in good spirits. They were constantly on the look-out for Scott's rival expedition, but still there was no sign of any other human presence. On 14 December they travelled the last 25 kilometres to the South Pole. There they each laid a hand on the pole holding a Norwegian flag and planted it together. They had scored a famous victory — a credit to their experience and endurance, but also to Amundsen's matchless organisation.

They remained at the Pole for two days, taking measurements and observations, and travelling around to make absolutely sure that they had indeed reached the correct place. They then put up a spare tent next to their flag and left a message for Scott, requesting him to inform the King of Norway of their achievement should Amundsen's party fail to return home.

They sped back over the 1270 kilometres to base without a hitch, reaching each of their supply depots as planned, and then Framheim itself — after a journey that had lasted a total of 99 days. It was 25 January, the very day that Amundsen had predicted for their return.

Amundsen's team spent two days at the Pole, taking measurements and making observations.

The Norwegian flag

Tragedy and afterwards

The hut built by Scott's expedition to Cape Evans (above and right) has survived more or less intact, and stands as a monument to the 'heroic age' of polar exploration.

Ponies in their stalls on the way to the Antarctic on board the *Terra Nova*

Travelling with ponies

'In my mind,' wrote Scott, 'no journey ever made with dogs can approach the height of that fine conception which is realized when a party of men go forth to face hardships, danger, and difficulties with their own unaided efforts... Surely in this case the conquest is more nobly and splendidly done.'

In fact, when Scott set out from McMurdo Sound on 3 November 1911, two weeks after Amundsen, his party of 16 men and 13 sledges also included 23 Siberian huskies and 10 ponies of a tough breed from northern China. The dogs, fed on fresh pony meat, performed well, but at the foot of the Beardmore Glacier they were sent back to base. The five remaining ponies were shot. Scott now continued with 12 men, and began climbing the Beardmore Glacier. They were still climbing it when Amundsen reached the Pole.

The great disappointment

Once on the plateau above the Beardmore Glacier, Scott selected the team to go to the Pole. He took with him, as planned, Lawrence Oates, Edgar Evans, and Edward Wilson, an enthusiastic naturalist who had accompanied him on his 1901–4 expedition. He also added to the team, at the last minute, Henry ('Birdie') Bowers. It was an unfortunate decision: there was not sufficient room in the tent for a fifth person, and Bowers was inadequately equipped with no skis. Bowers now began a laborious journey trudging a distance of over 500 kilometres on foot in deep snow.

Short of supplies and beginning to suffer from scurvy, the five men pushed on towards the south, dragging their sledge behind them. On 16 January, to their horror, they came upon the

The members of Scott's expedition line up for a group photograph, taken at the South Pole.

Scott and his party face their moment of bitter disappointment as they find Amundsen's tent and the Norwegian flag at the South Pole.

remains of Amundsen's camp close to the Pole, surrounded by dog tracks. The next day they found Amundsen's tent, flag and letter at the South Pole itself. The party were crestfallen. 'It is a terrible disappointment,' wrote Scott, 'and I am very sorry for my loyal companions.'

Dejected, Scott's party began the long haul home, hampered by a shortage of food and fuel, illness, worsening weather and their bitter disappointment. Evans collapsed in the snow and died, and Oates became seriously ill. One night, realising that he was hindering the rest of the party, Oates walked out of the tent into a blizzard, saying, 'I am just going outside and may be some time.' He was never seen again.

The end

Scott, Wilson and Bowers struggled north. By 22 March they were pinned down in the tent by the weather. Scott wrote in his diary: 'Blizzard bad as ever — Wilson and Bowers unable to start — tomorrow last chance — no fuel and only one or two of food left — must be near the end. Have decided it shall be natural — we shall march for the depot with or without our effects and die in our tracks.' In fact they were just 17 kilometres from a supply depot, but a week later they were still stuck in their tent. 'It seems a pity,' wrote Scott on 29 March, 'but I do not think I can write more.'

Manhauling in a blizzard in modern times

The remainder of Scott's expedition at base camp waited as the polar winter set in, suspecting the worst. In the following spring a search party set off along Scott's trail. On 12 November they discovered the tent; inside were the bodies of Wilson, Bowers and Scott, along with Scott's diary and film containing tragic photographs of the demoralized expedition at the Pole. In the race for the South Pole, Scott and his four companions had paid for their poor planning with their lives.

Amundsen returns

On 30 January 1912, Amundsen and his party left Framheim and rejoined the *Fram*, which set sail for Tasmania. Here he was able to announce to the world that he and his party had been the first to reach the South Pole. On his way home he stopped off in South America, where he wrote up a report of his journey, published under the title *The South Pole*. He eventually returned to Norway in 1913.

By this time the fate of Scott, his diary and the expedition's photographs, had been discovered. His story of ghastly suffering and tragic failure, of devotion to his country and the circumstances of his death, captured the public imagination. The press was less interested in Amundsen, who, thanks to his meticulous planning, had made the discovery of the South Pole look rather too easy.

In the nationalistic atmosphere of the years leading up to the World War I (1914–18) Scott made a good hero for the British. Newspapers made much of the fact that Amundsen had used dogs, whereas Scott's expedition had reached the Pole with the strength of their bodies alone. Worse, Amundsen had killed many of his dogs and fed the meat to other dogs; he and his colleagues had also eaten some of the dog meat, and even enjoyed it. This was portrayed as barbaric: it was as if Amundsen had somehow cheated and robbed Scott of the glory he deserved. The fact that Scott had shot his ponies and fed their meat to his dogs was conveniently ignored.

The result was that, in his lifetime, Amundsen — like Peary before him — was never accorded the respect and fame that he deserved. There is, however, no dispute about the discovery of the South Pole as there is over the North Pole. Amundsen made exhaustive calculations to ensure that his expedition had reached the Pole, and Scott's calculations also confirmed this.

Amundsen, photographed in Buenos Aires, Argentina, in 1912, before his return to Norway. The strain of polar exploration shows in this photo — he looks considerably older than his 40 years.

One person who did fully appreciate Amundsen's achievement was Peary himself. On hearing of Amundsen's success, he cabled the following message: 'Congratulations your great journey. Dogs are only motor for polar work.'

More polar exploration

Despite these setbacks, Amundsen's interest in the polar regions remained undimmed. In 1918, he set out for the Arctic in a purpose-built ship called the *Maud* and travelled through the Northeast Passage (see page 8) — becoming the first person to complete both the Northwest and the Northeast Passages. The crew of the *Maud* then attempted what Amundsen had planned to do in the *Fram* in 1910: to drift in the ice towards the North Pole. But the *Maud* (now without Amundsen on board) drifted to the north of Siberia and, after two years, the crew gave up.

Amundsen was one of the first of the older polar explorers to accept that exploration could be achieved more efficiently by travelling by air than on the surface. On 9 May 1926, the American pioneer aviator Richard Byrd claimed to have flown over the North Pole in an aeroplane. By this time large airships,

Richard Byrd (above). Byrd's plane (right) is unloaded in preparation for his Arctic flight in 1926.

called dirigibles, looked as though they had a future to rival the aeroplane. Just four days after Byrd, on 13 May 1926, Amundsen reached the North Pole travelling in a dirigible called *Norge*, piloted by the Italian, Umberto Nobile. On this day, Amundsen became the first person to have seen both the North and the South Poles.

Two years later, Nobile's dirigible *Italia* crashed in the Arctic. Amundsen volunteered to go in search of him, but on 18 June the aeroplane in which he was travelling disappeared, and Amundsen was never seen again.

The peoples of the Arctic

The first Eskimos

Whereas no people have ever settled permanently within the Antarctic Circle, various peoples have inhabited the far north for thousands of years. These include the Eskimo or Inuit of Greenland, northern Canada, Alaska and eastern Russia; the Chukchis and Yakuty of north-eastern Siberia; the Nenets to their west in northern Russia; and the Lapps of Scandinavia.

It may seem surprising that anyone would want to live in the frozen lands of the far north, but in the early history of the human race all peoples lived by hunting, and the Arctic offered unusual opportunities. It was rich in fish, seals, walruses, whales and sea birds. These animals allowed small communities of hunters to live successfully along the coasts of the Arctic north.

The first settlers in northern Canada arrived from Asia at least 10,000 years ago. At that time, during the Ice Age, sea levels were much lower because so much water had been frozen into the icecaps. As a result, Asia and North America were linked by land. These early peoples of the Arctic north made simple stone weapons and tools. In about 800BC they were replaced by settlers of the Dorset culture, who had more efficient ways of hunting. They used harpoons and kayaks — small, fast canoes made of skins and wood — and built igloos. After about 2000 years they, in turn, were invaded and replaced by people of the Thule culture, who spread eastwards from Alaska. These people were experts in hunting sea mammals, and used dog sledges.

As we can see from these archaeological remains, winter quarters for people of the Thule culture were strong huts built of stone, with a floor of turf placed over rafters of driftwood or bones.

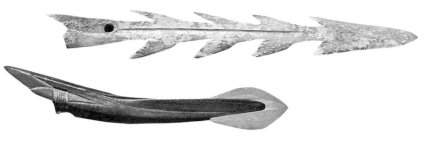

Eskimos used
harpoons with detachable
heads made of bone, ivory or
stone.

A hunting life

The Thule people were the direct
ancestors of today's Eskimos.
Most of these peoples
maintained their traditional ways
of life until about 50 years ago —
and some still do. Eskimos
hunted with spears, harpoons
and nets to catch seals,
walruses, narwhals and fish.
The harpoons usually had a
wooden shaft and a barbed head made of bone or ivory which
was attached to a long line. Once the animal was hit, the
harpoon head stuck into its flesh and the hunter could then haul
in the catch. Almost every part of the animal was used. Eskimos
ate fresh fish and meat, and carefully preserved quantities of food
to last through the dark winter. They made their clothes and
bedding from furs; they used the blubber (fat) of seals and
whales as cooking oil and burned it in their lamps; they used
animal bones to make tools, fish-hooks and hunting weapons,
and burned bones as a fuel.

During the summer months, Eskimo families travelled
hundreds of kilometres in search of prey. They lived in tents
made of skins placed over frames of wood, or sometimes whale
bones. They travelled on sledges drawn by their famous dogs,
the huskies, or in umiak boats which were big enough to carry
whole families as well as their possessions — clothes, bedding,
food utensils such as bowls made of wood and soapstone, and
hunting weapons.

The Eskimos, however, were not nomadic people. Each
winter they would try to return to their own village. Their winter
homes were usually shelters of
rock and earth, sometimes dug
into the ground, and roofed
with driftwood and whale
bone covered in turf. Each
house was occupied by three
or four families who would
have their own separate areas
within a single, large room.
They slept on low benches
made of a bank of earth, and
cooked over an open fire either
in the centre of the shelter, or
in a small room to one side. In
such conditions there was no
privacy. Eskimos lived close to
one another, and formed
tightly-knit families. During the
long winters, they entertained

Fish is allowed to dry in the summer sun,
then stored for use during the long winters.

Throughout history, many travellers have noted that Eskimo people are suprisingly cheerful, despite their hardships. They have a long tradition of parties, celebrations, jokes and storytelling.

Snow can be blindingly bright, even on dull days. Eskimo snow goggles — a wooden mask with narrow slits for the eyes — protected their wearer from the glare.

themselves with storytelling, games and parties and by carving weapons and ornaments out of ivory and bone.

The entrance to the winter house was a small door leading to a long, dipping tunnel, which helped to keep out the cold. It could be very snug and warm inside the house — so warm that Eskimos often stripped to the minimum of clothing. Light was provided by oil lamps.

The air would be thick with smoke from the fire, oil fumes and breath. Many early European travellers found this atmosphere quite unbearable.

Some Eskimo groups built large igloos as their winter homes. These, too, were very warm inside, despite the surrounding ice.

The art of building igloos has not been entirely lost. Today, these icehouses are used as temporary shelters during hunting expeditions. Warmer than tents, igloos were used as winter homes in the past.

Eskimos will wait for hours on end to catch a seal as it rises to take a breath at a small air hole in the pack ice.

Today, however, igloos are built only as temporary shelters during hunting expeditions in the summer. Experts can build an igloo in less than an hour.

The modern world

Not long after the first European explorers arrived in the Arctic, other ships followed to hunt for whales and seals, and to trade with the Eskimos. The Eskimos exchanged valuable furs for metal knives, guns, woollen blankets, sugar and whisky. It was the start of contact with the rest of the world which, over the centuries, completely changed their old patterns of life.

Today, most Eskimo communities have modern prefabricated homes, with oil-fired central heating, telephones, television and radio. The children go to school, and many of the adults have jobs in offices or factories, or at one of the oil installations which have been developed in parts of the Arctic.

However, over the last 50 years or so the disappearance of the traditional ways of life of the Eskimo peoples has started to cause concern. Many of the communities seemed lost in the modern world. There were growing problems with poor health, alcoholism, depression and suicide. In recent years great efforts have been by various communities to revive the traditions of the past and adapt them to the new conditions of Eskimo life. This is expressed in traditional crafts, such as carving. Inuit craftsworkers in Canada create beautiful carvings of Arctic animals out of soapstone, which fetch high prices. The Eskimos are also keen to maintain other traditions, such as their various languages, their diet of meat and fish, their old religious beliefs and legends. Many Eskimos still go hunting — if only at weekends. They may now use guns and snowmobiles, or boats driven by outboard motors, but their skills in hunting belong to a tradition stretching back over thousands of years.

The Lapps

Reindeer roam across the semi-frozen lands of northern Scandinavia, from the Kola Peninsula in Russia, across Finland and Sweden to Norway. This is also the land of the Lapps, or Sami as they call themselves. By the coast, many of the Lapps were farmers and fishermen, but inland some of them have lived for hundreds of years by herding reindeer.

As the reindeer migrate in spring, the Lapp herders follow the animals from their inland winter refuges to the summer pastures in the mountains or at the coast. Some of the reindeer are semi-tame, and can be harnessed to sleighs. The traditional home of the Lapp herders is a tent made of reindeer skin stretched over wooden poles, or in winter a set of poles covered in birch bark and turf. Few of the Lapps live by reindeer herding today, but the Lapps are proud of their heritage of survival in the Arctic north and still wear their traditional embroidered costumes with pride.

What happened later

In 1958, the world's first nuclear-powered submarine, the USS *Nautilus* crossed the Arctic Ocean beneath the ice. This is a record of the sounds of that journey.

Past and present: a modern snowmobile in Antarctica tows a sledge built to the design pioneered by Nansen over a century earlier.

The North Pole

Amundsen's belief in polar exploration by air set a pattern for the next 40 years. Why go through all the suffering of surface travel with sledges, if you can travel more quickly and comfortably in an aeroplane? In 1948, Pavel Gordiyenko of the Soviet Union became the first to land at the North Pole in an aeroplane, and therefore the first person definitely to reach the North Pole.

If the North Pole is in the middle of an ocean covered by ice, it must be possible to sail underneath the Pole beneath the ice. This was what USS *Nautilus*, the world's first nuclear-powered submarine, set out to do in 1958. It travelled from the Pacific Ocean to the Atlantic Ocean by going under the Arctic icecap, reaching the North Pole under the ice on 3 August. This voyage showed the efficiency of nuclear engines: the *Nautilus* went 200,000 kilometres 'on a lump of fuel no bigger than a baseball', as one member of the crew put it.

It was not until 1968 — 59 years after Peary's expedition — that the first person travelling across the ice reached the North Pole for certain. The American, Ralph Plaisted, and three companions travelled by snow scooters and received supplies dropped by aircraft along the way. The following year the British polar explorer Wally Herbert and three others made one of the last great journeys by dog sledge. They travelled with 34 huskies right across the Arctic Ocean, from Alaska to Svalbard, via the North Pole.

In 1977 a team from the Soviet Union showed that there was yet another way to do it. The Soviet icebreaker *Arktika* smashed its way through the surface ice all the way to the North Pole.

The South Pole

The era of Scott and Amundsen was known as the 'heroic age' of polar exploration, but it did not end in 1912. Ernest Shackleton returned to the south in 1914, intending to make the first crossing of the Antarctic continent. However, his ship, the *Endurance*, was crushed by ice in the Weddell Sea. Shackleton and the 26 members of his expedition stayed alive on the pack ice and eventually reached the tiny, deserted Elephant Island after spending four months in open boats. Now facing starvation and winter, Shackleton realised that he had to get help. With two others he set sail for South Georgia, 1300 kilometres away. He reached South Georgia after 16 days and raised the alarm. Several months later a steamer managed to get through the ice to rescue the men on Elephant Island — all of whom had survived.

Shackleton's plan to cross Antarctica was not realised until 1955–8, when the British Commonwealth Trans-Antarctic Expedition led by Vivian Fuchs crossed from the Weddell Sea to the Ross Sea. The expedition travelled 3475 kilometres, mainly by

Shackleton's ship, the Endurance (below and right), was crushed to matchsticks by the ice during his 1914 expedition. This led to one of the most heroic rescues of polar exploration.

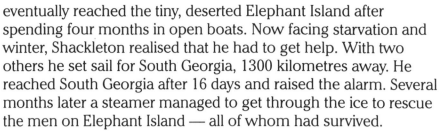

powerful tracked vehicles called 'snocats', and supplies were dropped from the air.

People have been flying in the Antarctic since the 1920s, and in 1929 Richard Byrd claimed to have flown over the South Pole. In 1956, Conrad Shinn, also of the USA, was the first to land at the Pole. Nowadays the large scientific station at the South Pole, called the Amundsen-Scott Station, has its own airstrip and is regularly supplied by air.

Large 'snocats' were used by the British Commonwealth Trans-Antarctic Expedition of 1955-8 to cross the continent from one side to the other.

The Antarctic Treaty

The polar regions remain two of the very few zones in the world which can be protected for the common benefit of everybody on our planet.

During the International Geophysical Year of 1957–8, scientists from many countries worked together in Antarctica and shared their knowledge. To encourage this kind of approach, the Antarctic Treaty was signed in 1959 by 12 nations who wished to promote peaceful scientific activity in Antarctica. The Treaty includes agreements about nature conservation, and protects the continent from potentially harmful activities such as military research and the dumping of nuclear waste. By 1994, 42 countries had signed the Treaty.

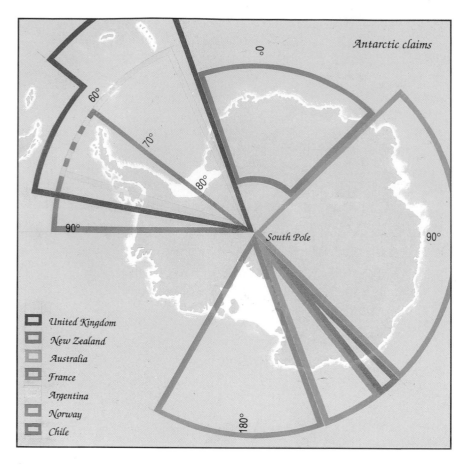

Antarctic claims

- United Kingdom
- New Zealand
- Australia
- France
- Argentina
- Norway
- Chile

However, the Antarctic Treaty may not provide protection for the continent forever. Maps of the Antarctic often show it sliced up like a cake to indicate the claims that various countries have made to the land. One day valuable minerals — such as gold or oil — may be found in the region; then these countries may no longer wish to support the Antarctic Treaty, and may wish to assert their claims to land.

The white ice of the Arctic may look pure, but traces of industrial pollution have been found in the blood of polar bears.

Nature in balance

Meanwhile, the harsh polar worlds have shown themselves to be fragile environments, in need of protection from human interference. The animals and birds that inhabit the polar regions survive because they have adapted to the conditions there, but these unique conditions can be easily upset by pollution, overfishing and imported disease. Scientists have found a hole over the South Pole in the protective layer of gas called the ozone layer in the earth's atmosphere. The ozone layer filters out many of the sun's harmful rays as they pass through the atmosphere. Air pollution from many parts of the world is drawn by air currents towards the Poles. This pollution has found its way into the food eaten by animals, and has even been traced in the blood of polar bears, and penguins' eggs.

In a small gesture of environmental protection, since 1994 huskies have been banned from Antarctica as part of a policy to remove all alien species to avoid introducing diseases to the wildlife of the region. (Human beings, however, are an exception to this rule!)

Exploration and science

Peary, Amundsen and others struggled to reach the Poles for the glory of it; nowadays almost all polar exploration has scientific objectives. In 1994, there were 44 scientific stations in Antarctica, run by 17 countries. These stations are staffed by scientists who come to study the geology of the continent, the movement of the ice, the weather, the wildlife, and the performance of the human body in extreme conditions. There are also scientific stations in and around the Arctic, some of them on ice floes.

Life is far more comfortable for these modern polar explorers than it was in the heroic days of Peary and Amundsen. They have specially designed, lightweight clothes made of synthetic fibres, snowmobiles, heated living quarters, satellite connections to the outside world, and air links to bring supplies and to help in times of emergencies.

Nevertheless, the polar regions remain tough and dangerous environments. Bitter cold can still cause frostbite and freeze engines, crevasses can swallow up people and their machines, blizzards and fierce winds can cause aeroplanes to crash, ice can still trap ships. These, at least, are problems that Peary and Amundsen would have understood well, because no polar explorers had greater understanding of, and respect for, the unique conditions at the far ends of the earth.

The sleek dome of the Amundsen-Scott base now stands at the spot where the race to the South Pole was won and lost. Flags of the Antarctic Treaty nations hang in the chill air.

Horizons

You could find out about these polar explorers: Naomi Uemura (completed first solo journey with dogs to the North Pole,1978); Douglas Mawson (expeditions to the Antarctic in 1912 and during the 1920s); Sir Ranulph Fiennes (Antarctic expeditions in 1980–1 and 1992–3); Will Steger (led the International Trans-Antarctic Expedition 1989–90).

Glossary

axis The line around which the earth revolves.

blubber The fat which forms a thick layer beneath the skin of marine mammals, and helps to protect them from the cold.

crevasse A very large slit or hole in the ice, found particularly in ice shelves and glaciers.

dirigible A large gas-filled airship, usually sausage-shaped, with an engine attached; passengers and crew could travel in a 'gondola' suspended beneath the airship.

Eskimo A general term for the various peoples of the Arctic and its perimeter, of Asiatic origin. Eskimo is a Native American word. The Eskimo peoples of Canada and Greenland prefer to be called Inuit.

frostbite A dangerous condition by which, in extreme cold, parts of the body become frozen and may be permanently damaged.

geology The scientific study of rocks.

glacier A large mass of compacted ice and snow which moves slowly under the force of its own immense weight.

husky A breed of tough dogs specially adapted to polar conditions, which can be trained to pull sledges.

iceberg A large mass of ice which drifts into the sea, usually after breaking off from a glacier or ice shelf.

icecap A vast, thick layer of ice, such as the ones that cover Greenland and Antarctica.

ice floe A large, flat raft of floating ice.

ice shelf A huge area of thick ice which permanently occupies large bays, and is attached to the land.

Inuit Eskimo peoples of Canada and Greenland. The word simply means 'people'.

latitude The horizontal lines, parallel to the Equator, into which maps of the world are divided. The Poles are at 90° of latitude north and south of the Equator.

longitude The vertical lines into which maps of the world are divided. The North and South Poles are at the points where all the lines of longitude meet.

manhauling Pulling sledges by human power alone, without the assistance of dogs, ponies or machines.

midnight sun The phenomenon by which the sun does not set at all during midsummer in the polar regions, giving 24 hours of daylight.

pemmican A nutritious preparation of dried meat or fish, mixed with dried vegetables and cereals. It usually comes in the form of hard, moulded cakes.

scurvy A serious disease caused by a lack of the vitamin C usually found in fresh fruit, vegetables and meat. Victims feel weak and tired, develop bleeding gums, and will die if not treated.

snocat A large tracked vehicle, similar to a bulldozer, used in modern polar exploration.

snowmobile A small motorised sledge, built like a scooter, driven by caterpillar tracks and steered by skis.

whaling Whale-hunting, usually conducted from specially constructed ships called whalers.

Index